Sacredness Surrounds Us in Every Season

CONTEMPLATIVE REFLECTIONS IN HAIKU
PRAYERS, PHOTOS, AND LONG POEMS

PATRICIA LEYKO CONNELLY

2023 First Printing

"Sacredness Surrounds Us in Every Season": Contemplative Reflections in Haiku Prayers, Photos, and Long Poems

All photos in this book were taken by Patricia Leyko Connelly. Any photos of the Weston Priory, or its grounds, were included in this book with permission of the Priory.

Cover and layout design by Paraclete Design, Brewster, MA

ISBN: 979-8-218-95350-8

10 9 8 7 6 5 4 3 2 1

Printed in the United States of America

"Attention is the beginning of devotion."

—Mary Oliver

"Instructions for living a life: Pay attention, Be astonished, Tell about it."

—Mary Oliver

"Nature is the direct expression of divine imagination."

—John O'Donohue

Contents

FOREWORD

Pat Leyko Connelly has long been attuned to what Jean-Pierre de Caussade calls "the sacrament of the present moment." Those of us fortunate enough to be familiar with her insightful haiku prayers and spectacular photos on social media have looked forward to them for years now for a daily dose of spiritual nourishment. Pat is one of those rare individuals who can see so much more than the rest of us in an ordinary tree or the routine experience of watching a sunset or the moon rising. She sees the hand of God. With this book, her engaging insights and keen eye for capturing the beauty of creation are available all in one place to help us to recognize the real behind the real. And we are spiritually richer because of it.

—Judith Valente, co-author of The Art of Pausing: Meditations for the Overworked and Overwhelmed *and author of* How To Live: What The Rule of St. Benedict Teaches Us About Happiness, Meaning, and Community.

INTRODUCTION

This book is a "Camino of the Heart" …my heart! It is a collection of prayers and photos and words that truly come from my heart, all in prayer and gratitude.

As a retired Music Minister, I found my spirit lacking expression. As a Benedictine Oblate, lay associate, I was settled into a somewhat contemplative lifestyle, and I needed to find my "way".

Taking walks, praying, and taking photographs became part of my new contemplative prayer practice.

Sharing my reflections with others online became a new kind of "ministry" for me. Seeing the Sacred and telling others!

Now, I share them here in this book in one place so that friends can pause and read, pray and reflect in their own time.

So, come, journey with me through the Seasons, which I believe surround us in Sacredness!

In gratitude,

Patricia

Prologue

Winter

Here, standing alone
Feet planted in winter's gift...
Sacred growth will come!

Spring

Trinity of blooms
Roadside blessings unfolding...
The gift of seeing!

Summer

Surrounded by green,
God's gifting to creation...
How can I not grow?

Autumn

Here in this moment
Feeling blessed by everything...
Sacredness surrounds!

Sometimes

Sometimes
You just need to look
a little harder, deeper and longer
to see the light.
You know it's there
You've embraced its faithful return
In the past.
Weariness might tempt you
to forget.
Sadness may distract your hopeful heart.
Don't let tears wash away
those signs of hope.
Brush away the clouds of doubt.
Be patient with all that is,
trust what is still possible!
Awaken your heart again.
Breathe in the breath of God
that sustains you!
Sometimes,
You just need to look
A little harder, deeper and longer
to see the light.
And believe,
It's there inside you, still.

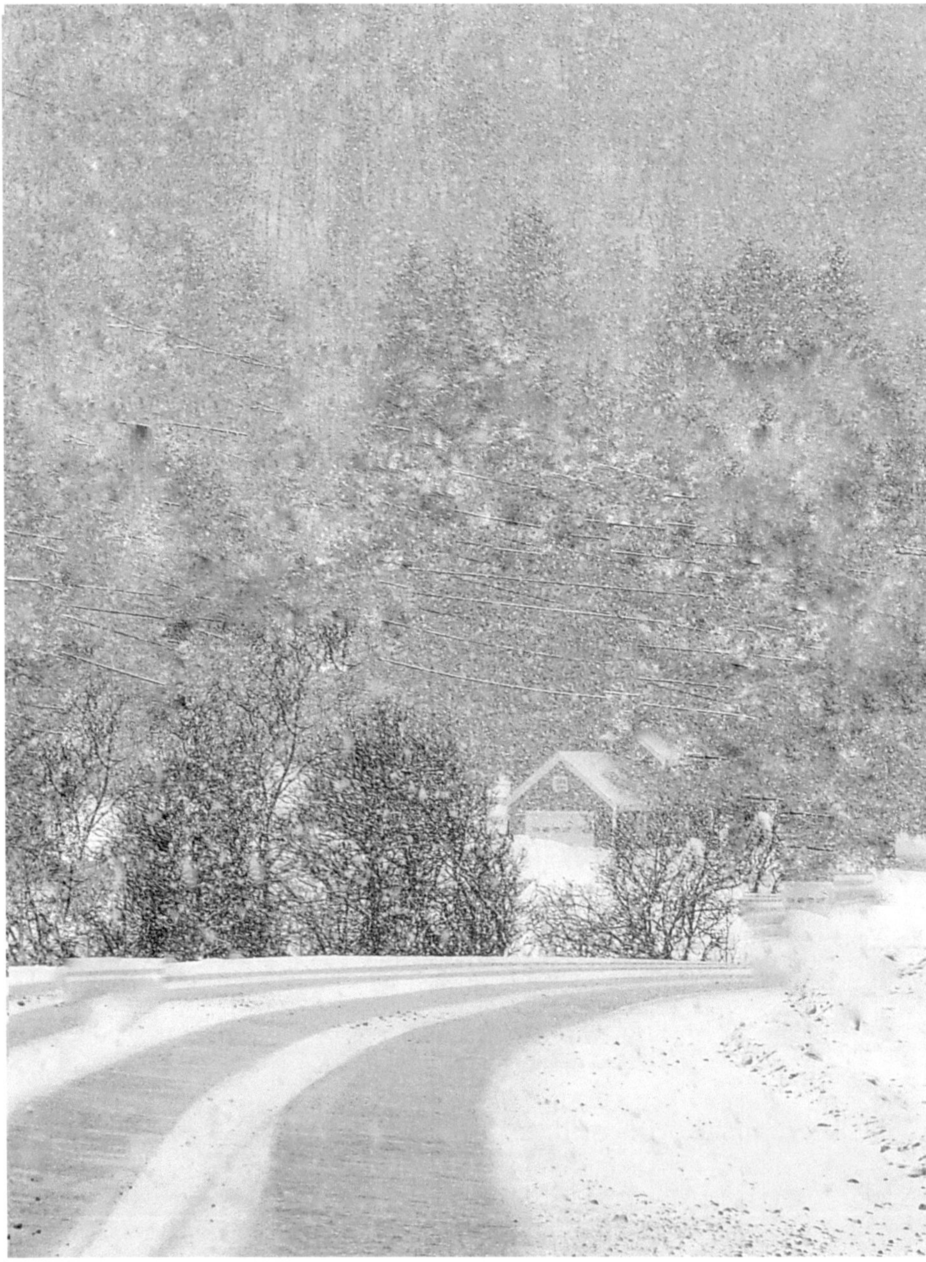

Winter

"When Winter Moves In"

Snow falling so hard
like lace curtains flowing from the sky.
"It's beautiful," I say.
As it blesses the air it passes through, the ground it falls upon!
Those beautiful bright winter days, those are the ones I dream of with blue sky and brilliant bright sun!
I go for walks, and the cold air chills my face and fogs up my glasses!
But it is beautiful, this winter, and it's refreshing to my soul and makes me feel alive! This cold air wakes me up to this gift of a winter wonderland!
Yet, now these days seem a bit more gray and cold and damp.
It's too cold to go out for those glorious winter walks.
Its seems as though Winter has "moved in" on this February day.
I stay inside curled up and warm with my cup of tea and book by the fire . . . a contemplative's dream!
I peer out my window now to empty streets of white and gray. No one seems to be "taking a hike" today!
So, I will stay in, secluded like a good Monk in her cell, silent and enjoying the quiet, cloaked in this warmth with the hum of the furnace that now sounds like "monk companions" chanting. I'm counting my blessings and trusting that Seasons do come and go!

Winter's light blesses
All who dare to be seekers…
Hope in all seasons!

"This Mood"

When winter weather
and my mood embrace.
Sometimes the day seems slow.

There is a comfort that I feel, in this quiet space.
The feeling of hurry seems to fade. I have nowhere to go.

Perhaps like the earth and all her creatures
it's time to rest, slow down, and pause
To take in all that has been
and dream of what has not!

A time to sit
and just be still…
like a Monk within her silent cell.

For we know that moods can come and go
Sometimes just like the weather
and a cloudy day can change and bring
An epiphany, new vision and new light!

The longer I gaze out my window
at this winter view, the more it is
like gazing at a Sacred Icon, those
Holy faces on my wall.

(continued)

(continued)

This window begins to reveal something new …
as I look with prayerful eyes.

My focus shifting from dark gray skies
to the promise of bright sun
Breaks through!

I'm so grateful for this time of resting,
Me and the weather here,
Together in this Winter mood.

In times of darkness
Know that a light shines for you…
welcoming you home!

Patricia Connelly 2023

"This Road ahead"

This road ahead …
I thought I knew …
I've traveled it before!

And yet, today, on this new day,
I seem to fear it so!

It looks so long with twists and turns,
trampled and treacherous too!
With my view unclear
I wonder now what lies ahead
on this road that I'm on.

Yet, when I stop and gaze a while …
Seeing footprints of those before me …
I imagine them and sense their presence—
I'm really not alone.

My eyes are opened
My footsteps hopeful.
A clearing and light to guide I now see.
The sign I needed.
God's surprising grace surrounding me!

I begin again,
moving forward …

On this road ahead!

Eve’ning Winter blues
The horizon, kissed good night …
Sacred is this Love!

"Snow falling softly"

Snow falling so softly
Whispering winter.
Not wanting to disturb the earth
The snow fell gently
Snow falling so softly
I almost missed its arrival
There was no sound
No
Just gift
Snow falling so softly
It even warmed my heart
Despite this weather's way
Snow falling so softly
trees covered in white
embraced as if by Angels' wings,
They welcomed this sacred seasonal kiss!
Snow falling ever so softly
And the earth stood still …
paused in silent reverence.
I bowed my head and softly prayed a Winter blessing.

"WINTER PAUSE"

Breathe in the stillness
Breathe in God's holy presence …
Breathe in, Be still … Be.

Take some time to gaze at the photo here.
Take a breath, be still, and experience this Sacred silence.
What would your Haiku prayer be?

(Write your prayer here or journal your thoughts.)

"In Night's stillness."

In night's stillness, I listen …
I hear the wind in the trees
the creaking of branches
Creaking like my bones!

In night's stillness I hear the sound
the whirling wind makes … like a lover's song
Lonely and longing.
I listen and wait for a reply.

In night's stillness I watch and listen.
I watch as stars appear without a sound
They arrive in this dark night like a monk
Taking their place in chapel, their prayer is silent.

In night's stillness, in my silent prayer, I make no sound …
I listen …

I know that in this stillness, the trees, moon, and stars, earth
creatures all, and our Creator are listening too!

Love is like moon glow
Ever waxing and waning …
Still, the light remains!

Earth and sky now one
Anointed in eve'ning grace...
God's sacred embrace.

Amidst clouds or sun
May we recognize Your Grace ...
In all its splendor!

Light of creation
Sacred gift that calls us all …
Come, lead us in Peace.

In my winter dream
Glorious sun warmed us all
Creation's blessings!

Trees in Winter's glow
Anointed in holy frost
Awaken my heart!

P.L.C.2022

"DREAM WALKING"

Walking, as if in a dream
one foot in front of the other
snowy road cushioning my way.

I breathe in the blessed freshness
of this winter walk,
feeling rested even as I journey.

Carrying with me questions and
ponderings that won't release me.
The silence of the forest sooths
my doubts and cradles my fears.

This tree-lined path opens up
as I offer myself in prayer
Birdsong is quieted
I pass the green rows of branch
like a silent Monk in procession.

Now, bright afternoon sunlight beams
behind two trees.
Its rays catch my eye and beckon me to stillness.
A patch of snow forms an imprint of a heart being held for me
to receive.

I notice, realize and bow.

Winter's gift calls us ...
In whisper or reflection
Come now and be still.

Pausing for Winter ...
Icy cold, still I remain
Blessings warm me now.

Silence speaks to us
Listening in deep quiet...
Hear what you long for!

To behold such gifts
Some visions frozen in time …
Dare to gaze at God!

In Winter's darkness
Gifts of light can still be found
Be still, Look, and see!

Spring

"Dreaming of Hope"

With dreams of Spring
Hope seems to be in the air.
Hope of flowers pushing their heads
through the once-frozen earth.
Snowbanks shrinking in the returning warmth of the sun!
Birdsong echoes through the trees
Their song now, not like solemn winter chants
This song is like a chorus of young monks happy to sing
their verse!
But this day we dream of peace.
Dream, if we can sleep.
A sleep that lets those dreams in.
Breath prayers whispered in and out, day and night.
Prayers still wet with tears.
Is there any other prayer now but for peace?
Do flowers and birdsong
or sun rays matter
If there is no Peace?
Spring still comes,
Awakening us to keep hope alive.
Spring still comes ...

Breathe in breath of love
Breathe out breath of God's own peace ...
Breathe ... Be still ... just Be.

With eyes wide open
Glimpses of Spring can be seen...
Gratitude's blessings!

Spring is persistent!
Reminds me to be patient.
And all shall unfold!

Bare trees now blossom
Brown earth opens to greening ...
Answering God's call!

When evening comes
Even the trees turn to You
Creator of all.

Melt my frozen heart
Release all that's closed, dead ...
Allowing new life!

Oh Creator God
You watch over all with love.
Heal and renew us!

Give us patience, Lord
As Spring waits for Winter's end ...
May we trust your ways.

Winter's gift passes.
God's blessings with each Season ...
Spring, we welcome you!

With arms open now
Forgiving dryness of heart ...
Grace will flow again!

This Season of hope
When flowers rise from dead earth ...
All is possible!

Reflecting God's love
Images we all share in ...
May we be that sign.

P.L.CONNELLY

The gift of each day
Blessed with hopes beyond our dreams ...
Continue to trust !

Monastics in chant
Dandelions processing ...
All in Praise of Spring!

LISTEN

Listening for your voice
You spoke many languages ...
Wind, rain ... all creatures.

"Soul Song"

Sing your song!
A sacred surprise sent by a Soul Sister or another simple Seeker.
A sweet sleepy-like Saint standing by your side. Silent but not small!
Smiling you into these simple melodies of the heart.
Sing!
Sing your soul song,
Simple and true
Sacred, Soulful surprise gift
that you are!
Sing!

Trees dance in the wind
Sacred birdsong fills the air ...
God's daily gifting.

In layers of love
God is surrounding us all ...
Receive it ... share it!

A Simple Poem / Prayer of Gratitude

The trickling of the nearby waterfall tells me we need rain.
The rustling of the tree branches and warm breeze tells me summer is near.
The sweet song of the birds from dawn to dusk reminds me that "All shall be well."
And this peaceful time of Gratitude tells me that God is near!

Spirit clouds above,
Lifting my eyes in prayer...
I am comforted.

Miracles appear!
The colors of spring bursts forth...
In humility.

Don't give up on hope
Blessings of light are for you
Trust they will return!

"Glimpses of Grace"

Like a game of hide-and-seek
We search for moments and signs
In hopes that Grace can be found.
Even just a glimpse.
Golden streaks bounce between the trees as I pass this
forest deep.
If I look away I can miss this gift in time.
Yet they are there.
I close my eyes and still my heart,
Memories of graced moments appear.
The song of birds in random harmony,
A gentle breeze or the howling winds remind me of psalm
tones I've chanted in prayer.
Dancing leaves applauding my arrival!
A smile, a touch, your voice!
That deep peace in Sacred silence.
Grace has found me!

Summer

"This Earth Monastery"

Here in this earth Monastery, trees surround me like
ancient Cathedral walls.
Birds chant daily prayers with me and teach me new psalms!
Creatures of the forest are my Monk companions.
The river streams along gently like holy water and the
fragrance of the pine trees is an offering of sweet incense in
their forest procession.
I walk gently on this holy ground, humming the whispered
ancient chants of the nights gone by … I breathe in peace.
Bowing in reverence and thanksgiving I pause; prayers rise
up through the clouds and to the starlit vaults above.
Heaven and earth joined as one.
Peace comes to this Earth Monastery.

A window of time
Sacred moments are revealed...
Grace beyond measure!

I gaze at the trees
Calling me deeper ... I go ...
Centered in God's peace.

"Gazing into God!"

Like a mystical staircase to heaven
I gaze into these cloudscapes
prayerfully imagining
that I am gazing into God.
The vision seems endless, like a quest that has no end. A
"Camino" of the heart!
I pause, almost like holding my breath
and I sense and know
that it is indeed God who is
Gazing at me!
I'm not alone on this journey. ..
What a miraculous gift to feel "noticed" and loved by God!

Listen, hear and see
The wonders of God's presence ...
Await us each day!

"DANCING CREATION"

The trees are dancing all around me!
Dancing in this summer breeze.

Music provided by a faithful choir of birds!
The hummingbirds add harmony after sipping from the nearby flowerbed.
And the bees and butterflies add to the dance, a dance they know by heart.

All is orchestrated by the Divine Maestro.
A masterpiece of creation!
The colors, sights, sounds, and smells of this earth fill up our senses.

This dance goes on day and night,
in season or out, whether I notice it or not.

I pray you don't miss it!

Summer's gifts abound
Offering colors, fragrance …
God nourishing

IN A MONKS GARDEN REFLECTING A PEACEFUL LIFE... SUNFLOWERS RISE UP!

In a Monk's garden
Reflecting a peaceful life ...
Sunflowers rise up!

In the quiet hours
With stillness of heart and mind ...
My spirit finds rest.

Sacred gifts of earth
Freely given and released ...
Bow in Gratitude

Illuminations
Breaking forth from a moonrise ...
Prayers in Sacred light.

Sacred earth and sky
Gifts of God's loving embrace ...
Send healing to this world.

"More to Give"

On a late summer's day
I sat in silence,
pondering what season my heart was in.
One single leaf fell from a nearby tree
And I felt like a part of me was dying.
Carrying my doubts I walked on...
there before me
was an old apple tree
looking weary and in need of rest.
There, spread out on the ground,
beneath tired branches,
lay the well-ripened fruits of her labor.
I've seen this tree in all its seasons.
Humility and wisdom flow like sap
through her veins.
And yet, she bowed to offer even more.
Surrounded by all of these gifts freely given ...
I still have much more to give!

Flowers grace my path
Summer crickets sing me home
I walk, not alone.

Heaven's symphony,
Divine music surrounds me...
Even in Silence!

SUMMER'S GIFTS ABOUND!

Summer's gifts abound
Offering colors, fragrance...
God nourishing us!

Autumn

AUTUMN'S HUMILITY"

Autumn can teach us humility.
If we are a willing student
and listen with our heart.
Just as creation seems to come to its fulfillment of growth,
Its fullness of beauty,
In that end of Summer's masterful beauty
just at the peak of each tree and each flower's calling,
comes the fading of the rose, the wilting of the daylily.
Autumn, you come and begin to teach us humility.
This lesson of life ...
God has blessed us,
we all have gifts to share and a fullness of life to offer,
you, Autumn, teach us that at some point ... there is a
Season of "letting go."
A Season of saying yes to "enough," yes to even death.
A Sacred season that teaches us humility, which can be
sweet if we accept it ... for there are fruits yet to bear.
We all must let go,
fall to the earth and die only to be reborn with the hope of
yet another Spring!

Leaves fall to the ground
Teaching us humility ...
Everything must change.

Living among trees,
They've become my "Patron Saints"...
Lessons of God's earth.

Heaven's Cathedral
The wonders of earth and sky ...
In Sacred presence!

And in this letting go,
Fear not and trust the process ...
... a Sacred season.

Take time to pause and reflect or write your own Haiku prayer.

In shades of Autumn,
The green fern turns brown and gold.
Your mys'try unfolds!

And I shall find rest
In the shadow of your wings ...
Surrounded by love.

I look, You are there
I seek and always find more ...
Opening my heart.

P L C 2021

Finding peace in change
Trusting that all shall be well ...
Seasons are Sacred.

Praying with the night
Sister moon guides heart and soul ...
Stars replace all words.

"Splendid Night Sky"

Oh, splendid night sky
I gaze at the heavens,
And Your sacredness surrounds me!
In evening's time of prayer and wonderment
I'm enfolded in your cloak of silence and star-shine.
In moonlight, whether half or full
light fills my being …
Reminding me of your presence around me.
Your constellations read like ancient psalms
I pray them nightly …
They guide my ways when I feel lost.
In the gaze of remembering
I see glimpses of loved ones gone before me
I smile at this starlight reunion!
I give praise and thanks to God
For all these lofty gifts … beyond my reach yet so near
…
I only need to look … and I am blessed!

When all is given
And your beauty is glowing ...
Know that Grace is here.

Take time to pause and reflect or write your own Haiku prayer:

These Seasons of life
Sacred moments passing by
God sent to cherish.

Moonglow, gift of night
Sacred Illumination
Giving praise to God!

I walk here in peace
Grateful for all that is peace ...
Praying for your peace.

When the changing of the Seasons
Starts to shimmer!

"A Cell without walls"

Monastic Sages say...
"Go and sit in your cell
And your cell will
Teach you everything."

In my contemplative cottage,
My Anchorage, my cell,
Autumn's Season of letting go and
Winter's call to enclosure and solitude
Offer sacred lessons for sure!
Now, Spring and Summer are birthing into full bloom ...

Come with me as I seek the wisdom from
My cell with no walls...

I am awakened by the days first light
the sun beams through the lush green trees like daytime fireworks!
Gentle birdsong floats outside my window
Back and forth like Monks chanting morning prayer.
Tiny yellow buttercups surprise me with smiles that spread wide across the open field...
A plethora of purple flowers appear like unexpected miracles!
A lone redwing Blackbird standing on a single branch, proudly chirps his familiar song by the riverside.
And a yellow butterfly lays still on the path reminding me how fragile life is!

(continued)

(continued)

Moments to cherish ...
Gifts of life's daily lessons.
Out under the brilliance of a blue sky who's end I cannot see and the warmth of the long-awaited golden sun that beckons me to wake up!
In the night hours, at my window I gaze up at the stars gathered in a blessed celestial community, they listen to my silent prayer.
All Sacred blessings, all gifts, all ready to teach me...if I'm ready.
Whether in my cell or on the road.

Gentle is the night
Daylight fades embraced in dreams
Hope in a new day.

This moment, this Grace.
Streaming down. This day, this time.
You surprised me Lord!

Made in the USA
Columbia, SC
06 December 2023

27212201R20100